Signs of
BLAVATSKY

TRIGUEIRINHO

Signs of
BLAVATSKY

An unusual encounter for the present time

Copyright © 2009 by José Trigueirinho Netto

The profits generated from sales of books by Trigueirinho are used for the maintenance of the Fraternity – International Humanitarian Federation and its affiliates.

Original Title in Portuguese:
SINAIS DE BLAVATSKY – *Um inusitado encontro nos dias de hoje*
Sao Paulo, Brazil: Editora Pensamento.
Copyright © 2009 by José Trigueirinho Netto

Cataloging-in-Publication Data
Trigueirinho Netto, José
Signs of Blavatsky : An unusual encounter for the present time Trigueirinho. – Second Edition, Mount Shasta, CA, Shasti Association 2020
ISBN: 978-1-948430-01-2
Library of Congress Control Number: 2017945325

English language rights reserved
Shasti Association
P.O. Box 318
Mt. Shasta, CA 96067-0318
editorial@shasti.org
ww.shasti.org

Contents

Publisher's Introduction	ii
To the Reader	vii
Helena Petrovna Blavatsky	ix

TOPICS

In a meeting for spiritual contacts	3
The dawn of Humanity	7
Something that Blavatsky expressed while incarnated	17
Our responsibility in facing what is to come	29
A life of contacts	39
The cosmic spirituality	49
The theosophical knowledge for the Future Race	55
New dharmic patterns after the planetary purification	63
Small fragments of the Great Silence	71

ADDITIONAL POINTS

Invisible worlds	85
The new Ten Commandments	87
Karma	91
Dreams, portals to the inner world	93

CONCLUDING TOPICS

An addition to the texts of Blavatsky	99
Seven paths open to the advanced human being	103
Bibliographical References	107
About Trigueirinho and His Work	109
Books by Trigueirinho	113

Publisher's Introduction

Blavatsky is the great occultist and initiator of a spiritual revolution that is still in progress today. If she were alive, what would she say to us? Some might respond that Blavatsky still "exists" and that we also, as little beings do not in fact die (is this not so?) and that great beings, as she was, only ascend to other levels of consciousness or dimensions of reality where they continue their work on behalf of humanity and the cosmos.

This was the belief of her personal secretary and compiler of the Secret Doctrine, G.R.S. Mead, who stated the following in his funeral oration to her:

"It is true that the personality we know as H.P. Blavatsky will be with us no longer; but it is equally true that the grand and noble individuality, the great soul that has

*taught all of us men and women to live purer and more unselfish lives, is still active"**

In the face of this truth, if we were to contact her could ask her a question, which is "what do you say to us now?"

This book offers an answer to this question.

José Trigueirinho Netto, the contemporary Brazilian spiritual philosopher and author, walks the fine line between the physical dimension and other more subtle worlds, sharing in his books, lectures, and recordings information that ascended masters and instructors as Blavatsky have to offer to terrestrial humanity. One could say, as a great Sufi mystic said centuries ago about herself, that Trigueirinnho "is eating the bread of this world and doing the work of the other world." With this ability he shares with us instruction that helps us to face the reality of today with spiritual wisdom, in alignment with consciousnesses that also instruct us and give meaning to our lives.

In the spirit of Blavatsky, who during her lifetime had the Mahatmas as her guides, Blavatsky 'reveals' herself here to Trigueirinho and a small group of students in her current name of "Enyalac", offering us a synthesis of her great spiritual teachings and advising us on how we might apply this knowledge in our lives now – an eternal knowledge or "Secret Doctrine" that is relevant to all times.

One may consider Trigueirinho himself in the tradition of Blavatsky, as a spiritual progenitor who has transformed lives, founded spiritual communities, supervised the foundation and development of monastic orders, and who served as a catalyst for a work of global service and prayer, announcing as Blavatsky did, the coming of a divine feminine energy to humanity in a form suitable to this epoch, age and to the spiritual needs of its seekers.

Even if this book does not come from Blavatsky – whoever she was, wherever she is, and whatever we might imagine that she might have to say to us now – Signs of Blavatsky can be considered as a product of her legacy. Thus we are invited to open ourselves to the message of these "Signs" and to the call that she sends to us so that we may live in service to the divine and in order that we may be the transmitters of spiritual light in this time of increasing darkness, in which humanity actions are destructive to the work of our Mother Earth.

Over 80 books of Trigueirinho are gradually being made available in English, along with his over 3,000 recorded lectures that are offered at no charge via the internet. By means of this great body of work he clarifies the reasons for the present crisis of planet Earth and announces a brighter cycle to come, teaching us that by contacting more subtle levels of consciousness and by assuming our real role in planetary evolution, we will avoid reacting negatively to an immanent natural catastrophe. Trigueirinho addresses issues related to: healing, a larger vision of astrology, the esoteric nature of symbols, sound and colors, the divine feminine, the emerging "New Humanity" and its Communities-of-Light, and about groups of service. He also speaks about topics often overlooked in spiritual teachings, such as the relationship of the humanity with the Animal, Vegetal and Mineral Kingdoms, and the negative group karmas derived from past actions such as slavery and the genocide against indigenous peoples. The work of Trigueirinho is a goldmine of significant revealing information on these and other topics.

His more than 40 years of ceaseless spiritual work has inspired the "Communities of Light" in South America and Europe as well as efforts of humanitarian service for the benefit of Nature, balancing in this way the karmas of humanity. All these initiatives are operationalized by means of the Fraternity International Humanitarian Federation.

This work from South America now arrives to North America just as Blavatsky herself came to us from Europe. The work of Trigueirinho enlightens us, enlivens us, and aligns us with the greater truths that when lived enable us to fulfill our purpose on Earth – truths that Blavatsky herself came to announce and which she served.

For more information on the work of Trigueirinho please consult the following websites:

The website of Trigueirinho: www.trigueirinho.org.br

Irdin Editora (publisher of the works of Trigueirinho and his associates): www.irdin.org.br

The Shasti Association (publisher of the books of Trigueirinho and his associates in English: www.shasti.org

*G.R.S. Mead as quoted in, WHEN DAYLIGHT COMES; A BIOGRAPHY OF HELENA PETROVNA BLAVATSKY, by Howard Murphet. Theosophical Publishing House, Wheaton, Ill, 1975, p. 252.

To the Reader

This book has come about after a deepened contact with THE SECRET DOCTRINE by Helena Petrovna Blavatsky (1831-1891). It benefits from the highly regarded biography of Blavatsky by Sylvia Cranston [1]. Our own impressions on Blavatsky's work have been added with the function of providing more unity to the texts.

Extracts from the writings of HPB are based on the Brazilian edition of her books and sometimes were translated in a more accessible way to current readers, without losing sight of the original vibration. Quotation marks were used to indicate these excerpts, freely translated into English. Thus, we hope to offer to the spiritual students a synthesis that will enable them to open new portals in consciousness in these times of intense work for the advent of the new humanity.

---

[1] HELENA BLAVATSKY, by Sylvia Cranston. Tarcher, New York, 1993

But, who was HPB?

A professor of Comparative Religions in Los Angeles answers us: "We don't know. Probably we will never know. She remains a noble mystery. (…) No one would leave the magical circle of her company without being changed. Even today, those of us who have come close to the flame she helped to light have been immensely touched by the grace that comes from her inspiration."

In a previous task HPB was called Upasika which, according to Helena Roerich, means *Disciple*. Currently, her task in the inner planes attunes her to the name Enyalac, and so we will call her this some of the time in these writings.

Trigueirinho
2009

Helena Petrovna Blavatsky

Writer who in the XIX century deepened the connection between science, religion and philosophy. Although not understood by most of her contemporary human beings, she was a scholar of ancient wisdom. She built a philosophical-spiritual legacy of inestimable value for the present days, which protects the essence of the esoteric thought.

Isis Unveiled and *The Secret Doctrine* are two of her works of evident superior inspiration. The bases for the future humanity are placed in it.

TOPICS

In a meeting for spiritual contacts

At 11 o'clock AM on the 9th of April 2009, a small group gathered, while in contact with inner levels of consciousness, to update some issues related to the services provided by Figueira, a spiritual center in the Southeast of Brazil.

On his way to the meeting, in the car, the author of this book perceived the presence of Enyalac (another name of HPB), which accompanied him from the subtle planes, but remaining invisible to the other occupants of the vehicle.

At the same time, a connection with the Temple of Ibez, a nucleus of consciousness active in the supra-physical planes of Central Brazil, was also made. Along with other tasks, Ibez enables the real transformation of the humanity living on the surface of the planet, starting with a reform of sidereal magnitude of the genetic code.²

At the beginning of the meeting we could see hovering over the group in the astral plane a great symbolic hand, from which fell silver and gold coins of energy. They disappeared upon reaching the floor.

We could understand that a new task was being announced to this group that had gathered. We perceived the presence of Antuakh, a member of the Planetary Hierarchy, accompanied by Enyalac and Rishkamel (the spiritual name of Mother Teresa of Calcutta). To the clairvoyant vision, Rishkamel appeared in a more youthful body than the one known from her photographs. Her garment was green with golden stripes. Rishkamel glided behind the group, which was seated in a circle, thus passing by all those who were present.

As the group began to sing mantras, there appeared to the inner vision another being, with a great book in its hands. It was Moses, with a long beard, dressed in an ancient style. He was accompanied by two other beings. The book he carried had an aged appearance and radiated a golden glow.

---

2 New genetic code: See ERKS- The Inner World and MIZ TLI TLAN-A World that Awakens. Note: For books of Trigueirinho that are cited in the text, complete information is available beginning on page 113.

As each being manifested internally we could confirm their truthfulness by projecting on them universal symbols appropriate for this purpose. The cross with two arms of the same length is one of these, since it represents perfect cosmic equilibrium. If true, the presence becomes clearer, brighter and more stable. In the event that it is not authentic, it will dissolve itself or reveal its real form. This could be an artificial creation or even an interference of negative forces.

The book of Moses had numbers from one to ten, one under the other. Enyalac continued to be present and also held a book in her hands, inside of which were several other smaller books. Enyalac came closer to Moses and both of them positioned themselves right before me. Then, from the center of the circle came a strong wind, and the pages of both books began to move rapidly. Rishkamel approached, and then the books turned into one. At this point Rishkamel held the new book and brought it to me.

Some interferences tried to insert themselves into the mental field of those present, but Enyalac and other beings who had also approached continued sustaining the meeting. Then the group began to work with specific symbols to dissipate all interferences. Right in the first symbol, in the very center of the group, opened in the etheric plane a special type of energetic tube that led to another kind of space.

One of those present began to have a clear consciousness of this space unknown to us, and Enyalac clarified that special conditions would have to be created for the proposed work to be carried out. Following this, I perceived that the group was being transferred to Ibez in their astral bodies. In a large room of stone, everyone stood up, forming a circle. Inside the circle was Enyalac, who spoke to us. She took, one by one, blank pages from a notebook that she was holding in her hands and handed them to each of us. We understood that we must be like those blank pages in order to impress in ourselves the inner instruction and to bring about in our lives new opportunities of service and development.

In that moment in my mental screen appeared a new book that opened itself. It was ancient. And, without words, Enyalac transmitted to me: *"Write down what you understand, whatever comes to you."* I started to make notes.

The dawn of Humanity

The human being appeared on the surface of the Earth during a period of transition between cycles of the universal evolution. Humanity is the result of a special cosmic process and because of this brings with it the hope of finding and revealing new vibratory keys which are necessary today for the improvement of the whole human race, that exists in different planes and dimensions in the entire universe. Over time, humanity - intentionally or by accident–continued to develop resistance to the tests that this project presented to them.

In the course of this process, it also happened that the humanity of the surface demonstrated signs of its importance within the Universe, which is one of the reasons why it still remains. Humanity is an experience that can generate new possibilities for racial composition, applicable to other systems, beyond the terrestrial one. Part of the history of the evolution of human beings, as recorded step by step since the beginning work until this day, is guarded in Ibez. It awaits the appropriate moment to unveil itself to the most wary members of the humanity of the surface.

The true history of humanity cannot be handed down to only one group of beings, even if its members consider themselves to be honest representatives of humanity as a whole. And for this reason also not even the great representatives of the Hierarchy had access to the totality of the historic and pre-historic codes. In these times of transition when we can anticipate deep changes in the planetary physical structure, the possibility of access to this kind of information is being re-evaluated, and the result will depend to a large degree on the response of human groups from the surface in complying with the Plan of Evolution.

For a group to receive part of this information, it must include representatives of various currents of spiritual knowledge. This possibility has been in preparation for a long time and today it approaches the souls destined for this task.

We were under the impression that the book shown by Enyalac contained part of the history of humanity; that it had several volumes and that what was offered to us now was a kind of prologue to this vast Work. If there was a response from certain human beings, the book would be continued.

Now, with the consciousness again focused on the meeting room, we saw that Enyalac was trying to move close, this time dressed as HPB, who was incarnated from 1831 to 1891. She embraced that book and stayed on the outside of the group, observing us. Later she brought her book, and Moses brought the one with ten numbers. And the book of Moses was included in the book that was with HPB.

Since the Ten Commandments until now have not been generally lived by humanity, it will be necessary to join them to other modern texts and form a single book. Moreover, we had the impression that the highest meaning of the Commandments was about to be revealed. It is important, at the present time, to encounter the Ten Commandments in their true form. Since their revelation to humanity, they have not always been well understood. On several occasions they were manipulated and translated according to various types of interests.

Some clairvoyants have already had visions of them in the *Akasha* (the universal etheric field where everything is registered), visions that have not always confirmed what is commonly known. However, it is always necessary to be cautious, because visions from the *Akasha* also run the risk of being altered, even involuntarily, by the still imperfect receptivity of the clairvoyant.

While incarnated, HPB skillfully expressed the capacity to perceive other levels and to channel information coming from the Hierarchies, whom she called Masters. On the other hand, in THE SECRET DOCTRINE, she clarifies: "Whatever the author does will never satisfy both Truth and Science. To offer the reader a systematic and uninterrupted vision of the *Archaic Stanzas* is impossible". And she continues: "They, the *Archaic Stanzas,* teach beliefs in Powers and Conscious Spiritual Entities, in semi-intelligent terrestrial forces and in highly intellectual forces from other planes, whose intellect is of a totally different nature from that which we can conceive on Earth. They are beings that live around us, in spheres which neither the telescope nor the microscope have the ability to reveal."

HPB explains that the true scholar, who she calls an occultist, believes in the *Masters of Light* and believes that the Sun, far from being just something which lightens up our days, "is like millions of other suns that exist in the Cosmos, a dwelling place or vehicle of a God, or of a legion of Gods."

The Sun is matter, but it is also spirit, like the cosmos, which besides having shape has a soul. However, "materialism and skepticism are evils that will subsist in the world as long as man does not transcend the present gross form to return to the one that he had in preceding races, in other stages of the Earth."

"Unless the skepticism and our natural ignorance of today are balanced by intuition and by a natural spirituality, all beings anguished by feelings of this kind will not see in themselves but a cluster of flesh, bones and muscles, with a hollow chamber within, which serves to store feelings and sensations." This is why the Light of the Spirit is the eternal place of seeking for the mystic and the searcher, who are little preoccupied with the limitations of the material senses. They rely on the inner senses or on other forms of contact with more elevated planes of consciousness.

With respect to science, it is far from the solution to the existing difficulties, unless it enters in relation to occult immaterial reality, and even with Alchemy, which is improbable today. It is not possible to disregard the intuition of the mystic in the face of the reality hidden within dense matter. On the other hand, according to HPB, there are intelligent workers who invisibly manage the solar system. But who are they? Physical science knows little about these beings and about certain forces, and the fusion of the two sciences, the archaic and the modern one, requires before anything that we abandon current prejudices and materialistic trends.

We acknowledge, therefore, the need to present a summary of information that will bring closure to an important stage of the Teaching, so that we may, before an inspiring source such as the intelligent contacts with extra-terrestrial and intra-terrestrial consciousnesses, prepare ourselves for the demanding tasks of today.

At the present moment no incarnate being is prepared to be a Spiritual Hierarchy to the full extent, but what does exist is the possibility to form groups of individuals that will act as channels for the Hierarchy. If a group of souls well-connected with the spirit permits an internal instructor to teach them, it may be possible to materialize the Planetary Centers[3], these conductors of cosmic energies to Earth. However, such internal instructor will not be on the physical plane, but will belong to the Hierarchy of

---
[3] Focal points of the universal energy on the planet, for they act based on supramental planes. The main centers at this time are: Anu Tea, Aurora, Erks, Iberah, Lys-Fatima, Mirna Jad and Miz Tli Tlan.

these centers. Some Intra-terrestrial Retreats[4] still unknown to the great majority of humanity may arise and unveil previously unknown truths, as the custodians of this information. But human beings would have to be prepared to absorb great blows to their ideas, as these revelations constitute a great challenge to even the most brilliant of minds.

In planets like Jupiter, for example, there is a fully pure science which contains revelations about the mechanism of the functioning of the universal mind, also called *Mind of the Creator*. All this indicates that if the Earth becomes a part of the Confederation of Evolved Worlds, it will not be able to remain as it is, and that some terrestrial beings must enter into deep retreat for a great part of their lives to be able to know and experiment, for example, another kind of *time*, different from the chronological and aligned to the energy of Omnipresence[5].

As we know, to reach deep retreat and the silence of contemplation, conditions necessary for the knowledge of certain truths, we need to accept certain steps that lead to inner union, and, therefore to the alignment with the spirit and the higher planes:

---

4 Nuclei that exist in a coordinate of the real time of the universe. They keep information that awakens us to other planes of consciousness.
5 Ninth cosmic ray—one of the fundamental energies of the cosmos. See ESOTERIC LEXICON

- Worship and continuous obedience to the Laws of Creation.
- Physical silence and, most of all, mental silence.
- Non-predominance of the influence of the individual being, enabling the possibility of using forces that facilitate a universal, Higher Service.

It is never too much to repeat that we need to be pure in our thoughts, actions and words and thus imagine ourselves united to the Brotherhood of the Cosmos dedicated to the evolutionary task. In this process, we will have to ignore ourselves as individuals and consider ourselves as a group, forgetting, however, past lives and all the negative marks left by them. After abolishing from the memory these experimental lives, we must surrender to the energy of Liberation[6] an immaterial energy closest to those who intend to take decisive steps in this evolutionary cycle.

Everything will depend on groups uniting themselves in one sole body and, in purity of intention, receiving the instructions that are currently available to humanity. These groups of souls will not be dissolved after accomplishing each phase of their work, but will unfold bringing living knowledge to other

---

6 Twelfth cosmic ray—one of the fundamental energies of the cosmos. See ESOTERIC LEXICON.

situations, each one broader and broader, and acquiring conditions to receive ever expanding evolutionary tasks.

Such scope is for us, today, something unimaginable. There is much to learn, and the studious shall appear. Sound, for example, as an occult force has unknown potentiality, and the groups must learn how to use it. It is said in *The Secret Doctrine* that it is possible to produce sound of such nature that not even the electricity generated by one million Niagara Falls could deter it. One can produce a sound that may lift in the air a pyramid such as the pyramid of Queops; a sound that may re-animate dying persons restoring their vigor and energy, as well as restoring vigor and energy to those who have exhaled their last breath.

But the work of HPB also highlights that indifference leads our epoch to only adore the biblical Calf of Gold, and that the History of the planet and of humanity is told with few scruples in face of the tradition, of the legends and of the myths. But it is through the legends and myths that one can encounter, symbolized, the true History. HPB says: "While materialism denies everything in the Universe, except matter, archeologists attempt to demean antiquity and destroy every assertion of the Ancient Wisdom, falsifying even chronology."

Thus, knowledge remains unrevealed and will only be recovered by means of supraphysical contact and alignment with living worlds in other planes of consciousness, beyond the three dimensions of the concrete world.

Something that Blavatsky expressed while incarnated

"I can only show the path to those whose eyes are open to the Truth, whose souls are full of altruism, charity and love for all of Creation, and who think of themselves only as a last thought."

Therefore, what HPB wrote as instruction was a small part of the knowledge at her disposal. She was selective about what she bequeathed us, to avoid greater misunderstandings beyond those naturally brought about by her unusual work. Her respect for human limitations and her consequent care were evident:

"It is not required that any one person carry a load heavier than the person can stand, or do more than it is possible… One bound to a duty in one place does not have the right to abandon it to attend to another duty, even if it is greater than the first one, because the first rule taught by occultism is that one should perform one's duty without giving it up for any other."

With all this, no one should feel bad for not understanding something. Excess of Truth could confuse and disturb the mind of a student, and also disturb compulsory karmic situations that must still be dealt with. "If people, because of circumstances or status in life, find it impossible to fully serve in this lifetime, then these persons should prepare their mind for the next time, in order to be ready to attend to the first call when born once again."

On the other hand, it is good to have in mind that, because of the conditions and opportunities at present—a time of transition—we can experience quick and intense processes, as if we were living several incarnations in the same life.

HPB also explains another of the reasons why she could not reveal all that she knew: "It is impossible to use spiritual forces if there is even a minimal touch of egoism in the future operator. Because, unless the intention is entirely pure, the spiritual will becomes psychic, and will act in the astral plane, and from this there may be terrible results. The powers and forces of the animal nature can be used as much by one who is egoistic and seeks vengeance, as by one who is altruistic and forgives everything; but the powers and forces of the spirit will permit being used only by those who are perfectly pure at heart..."

In *THE VOICE OF THE SILENCE*[7], a book published for the first time in 1889, HPB clarifies: "The human being is, internally, a crystal ray from the universal soul, an immaculate beam of light and, externally, a clay form. This ray of light is the guide of its life, and its real Self, the Guardian and silent Thinker."

Many were sorry that the members of the Spiritual Hierarchy did not reveal certain knowledge, being strict in transmitting information. For example, the existence of intelligent beings in our Solar System and outside it was always a piece of information left intentionally incomplete, a mere mention without detail. With regard to this, HPB affirmed that "neither the symbols nor the numbers can be transmitted to the public, and numbers and symbols are the keys to the esoteric system." The same also applies to certain information about the Unknown.

---

[7] THE VOICE OF THE SILENCE, by Helena P. Blavatsky. Theosophical Publishing House, Wheaton, IL 1982.

She even transcribed part of a letter from one of her Masters in which he affirmed the difference between knowledge obtained from others and Wisdom. While knowledge and external information represent the thought of others, Wisdom comes from the individual's own soul.

In this way, we are given a key that indicates the necessity to search for ourselves, internally, and not to stay forever conditioned to someone else's thoughts, no matter how good they seem to be. "Students, have perseverance, as those who have to persist eternally. Your shadows live and fade away; but that which in you will live forever, that which in you KNOWS, is not of the fleeting life", says *The Voice of The Silence* in verse 138.

And what is the Universal Spirit and the Supreme, the One and Only Spirit, so present in the writings of HPB? It is the essence that sustains and animates all of us and all that exists. It is unity, the origin of all life. But "the Spirit is shapeless and immaterial, and when individualized in a man, it is made of the most elevated substance. Thus, the individual spirit is part of the Universal Spirit, individualized by its union with a physical form. It is not a formal entity, for where there is a form there is cause for pain and suffering"—and the Spirit is above this.

It is necessary not to confuse spirit with soul. In the same way as matter is a field for the manifestation of the soul in our level of existence, the soul is a vehicle in a higher plane for the manifestation of the Spirit. "Therefore", says HPB, "spirituality is an immaterial concept of things and of life. It leads us to experience by *living* that everything that exists is animated by the Supreme and Universal Spirit. We see that spirituality is not religion. The religions conquered converts with the tip of the sword and built temples over enormous massacres of human lives. History was falsified, and facts intentionally distorted; fanaticism and materialism prevail in it—one that is all-accepting and the other that is all-negating. Spiritualists are those who keep serene between these two extremes and who trust the eternal justice of things."

There is an ancient and universal wisdom that was known to some, and which has gradually been altered over time. HPB says that "some fragments escaped geological and political cataclysms to tell their history; and what was saved demonstrates that the Secret Wisdom was in ancient times the only source, the perennial and inexhaustible source from which all currents were fed—the subsequent religions of diverse peoples, from the first to the last one." But many who were at the head of religions betrayed the sources, led by hidden interests or even by human ignorance.

HPB reaffirms one of the sources of her work: "We have been supported by Hermes and the Hermetic Wisdom, in its universal nature; science leans on Aristotle, against intuition and the experience of the centuries, imagining that truth is the exclusive property of the Western world." And, from then on, the spreading of history began to be degraded, which invites us to trust exclusively in our own inner voice. "Have patience, Candidate, as one who does not fear failure or bow to success", as says this voice and as it is transcribed in verse 137 of THE VOICE OF THE SILENCE. "But we need not wait long; many of us will see the dawn of the new Day, at the end of which many debts and differences between races will be resolved."

Is this moment near? Are the many signs that we are receiving today speaking about this? In the face of so much politics between religions and so much distortion of the Universal Laws, that should be known to the peoples, is this the case of agreeing with the philosopher who said: "There is only one true religion, which is the worship of the SPIRIT OF GOD"?

An ascended master wrote to HPB: "Do not share with the present generation the great Truths that constitute the legacy of the future Races. (...) Be prudent, we repeat, prudent and wise, and above all, be careful to assure yourself of that which those who listen to Our teachings believe in, so that in deluding themselves, they will not delude others."

In the face of this, we should ask ourselves: When will we be a trustworthy humanity? When will we walk with more sincerity and safety on the surface of this planet? These are questions that, if considered, could speed the inner rhythms of those who are well-intentioned. "...the solitary Pilgrims, whose feet bleed on their way back to their Homeland, will never be safe, until the very last moment, of not losing their path in this limitless desert of illusion and matter that is terrestrial life."

We can see that we had already been mature for some time, we, who need something more perfect in our lives, to be aware of the existence of other levels of life, on this very Earth still not consecrated. So the Hierarchy began to prepare systems of internal communication between the human beings from the surface and the intra-terrestrial and supraphysical beings. The Planetary Centers began to be revealed, and their location for contact on the physical plane started to be manifested. First Erks, Miz Tli Tlan, Aurora, Mirna Jad, Lys-Fatima and, in the end, Iberah and Anu Tea.

To consciously enter into this evolutionary stream, privileges do not exist. THE SECRET DOCTRINE teaches clearly that "there are no privileged beings in the Universe, neither in our system nor in others, neither in the external worlds nor in the inner worlds—privileged beings such as the Angels in the Western religion or Judaism. Archangels do not arrive or are born as such on this plane of existence, that is, like a completely developed angel; but all Archangels *become what they are.*" And continuing, HPB reveals: "The Great Kings ended, in previous periods, their cycle on Earth and on other worlds. In future manifestations they will be lifted to systems superior to our planetary world, and their place will be taken by the chosen ones from our humanity, the precursors on the difficult and strenuous path to progress."

Are they, these future predecessors, among us, humans of today? Yes. "The humans of our own cycle of life will be, in the next great period of manifestation of the universe, which consists of several stages of billions of solar years, the instructors and guides of humanity whose Monads[8] may now be imprisoned—

---
8   Nucleus of consciousness that is fundamental in the present phase of evolution of the human being. It is the imperishable center of the life of humankind. See ESOTERIC LEXICON.

semiconscious—in the most intelligent specimens of the animal kingdom, while their inferior principles may enliven the most developed members of the plant kingdom."

"From the highest Archangel to the last conscious Great Constructor, all these are humans that lived in past eons, in this or another spheres; and the inferior elementals of today, semi-intelligent or unintelligent, are all future human beings."

"The being acquires intelligence during the human cycle. One cannot possess consciousness or human intelligence without acquiring it individually."

Right away, in the first Volume of THE SECRET DOCTRINE[9] we read: "The entire order of Nature testifies that there is a progressive journey that leads to a superior life. There is a plan or design in the action of forces, even in those which appear to be the blindest. The whole process of evolution, with its endless adaptations, is proof of this. The immutable laws that eliminate the weak species to give place to the stronger ones and thus assure the survival of the fittest, although cruel in their immediate action, cooperate in every sense with the great final goal.

---

[9] THE SECRET DOCTRINE—The Synthesis of Science, Religion and Philosophy, Volume I, by Helena P. Blavatsky. Theosophical Publishing House, Wheaton, IL 1993.

The very fact that adaptations occur and that the fittest are the ones that survive in the struggle for existence demonstrates that what is called *unconscious nature* is, in reality, a complex of forces managed by semi-intelligent beings (elementals) under the direction of advanced Planetary Spirits. Where is the one who would dare to deny a self-consciousness in the plant or even in the animal? All that one can say is that this consciousness transcends the limits of understanding."

But one of the most significant points in the message of HPB is found in the necessity to adjust our energy of devotion:

"Neither the collective legion nor any of the forces that act, considered individually, deserve honors and divine cults. All of them deserve, however, the reverence and the gratitude of humanity; and humans must always make an effort to aid the divine evolution of ideas, becoming, according to their resources, collaborators of Nature in its cyclical task."

And she summarizes, without leaving place for doubts:

"Only the CAUSE WITHOUT CAUSE of all things must have its sanctuary and its altar in the sacred and inviolable enclosure of our heart, invisible, intangible, unmentioned, except by the quiet and silent light of our spiritual conscience. Those who worship it must do so in the tranquility and sacred solitude of their souls."

Our responsibility in facing what is to come

"It may be that the minds of contemporary generations are not mature enough to receive occult truths. It is very possible that this will be the conclusion of advanced thinkers of the future Sixth Race[10] when they look back over the history of full and unconditional acceptance of the Esoteric Philosophy. Until then, the generations of our current Fifth Race will continue to lose themselves through the hidden chambers of preconceptions and prejudices."

HPB lived during the full advent of scientific ma-

---

10 We consider, with Theosophy, that there are seven human Races since the human being has appeared on this planet. Four of them have already lived and the Fifth one has to complete its terrestrial cycle. Two still have to appear: the Sixth and the Seventh ones. The course of these races corresponds to great periods of evolution, many millions of years. However, in the chapter "Life, Races and Cycles" of the book UNVEILED SECRETS we expanded the numbers of races but due to reasons described there—not in disagreement with the classical doctrine spread by HPB.

terialism and today the situation does not seem to have changed—on thecontrary, materialism continues expanding. She adds, in another section of THE SECRET DOCTRINE, that we are at the peak of materiality: "The animal tendencies, although more refined, are nonetheless not less nimble, which one can observe, principally in the civilized countries." However, all ancient teachings affirm that "the first human group emanated from the very essence of superior semi-divine beings, and therefore were very advanced. But Nature," continues HPB, "in the present state of evolution, no longer employs such a process. While in extremely remote ages there were humans and civilizations in a certain sense much more advanced than today, now there is a spiritual, intellectual and animal evolution—but the Creative Forces governing the races are the ones who now construct the physical form and compel their evolution towards perfection." This, according to HPB, is at the price of an equivalent loss of spirituality.

But there has been a turning point, and lately "it is the higher self of the human being, or the reincarnating principle, that rules over the animal ego, and governs it, whenever the latter does not drag down the former. Now spirituality is in its ascending arch, and the animal or physical aspect only makes the normal progress on the path of evolution difficult when the egotism of the personality contaminates the inner being, in such a way and so strongly, that the superior attraction loses all its reign over the thinking and rational being."

We see, if we observe well, that those who are the simplest human beings are the ones who are more open to the mysteries of the Evolutionary Plan. However, it may be said "that vice and evil constitute an abnormal and unnatural manifestation in the present stage of the human evolution—or so it should be. The fact that humanity has never been more egotistic and vicious than today, because civilized nations have even managed to make egoism into an ethical characteristic, and vice into an art, is still more evidence of the exceptional nature of the phenomenon."

The Secret Doctrine reveals that our current race, the Fifth, is closer to what one could call interstellar ether—and thus becomes less material than before and tends more to psychology than to physics. "The pineal gland is much more related with the soul and with the spirit than with the physiological senses of humanity." We are on our way to the total development of the senses of the mind and the intuitive omniscience of the soul. This, without mentioning the hindrance that matter can produce.

In the still very distant Seventh Race, there will be three types of human beings: white, yellow and African Negro with their respective inbreeding. According to HPB, those who will be extinct are the redskins, the Eskimo, the Papua, the Polynesians and others. They will be extinguished gradually, abandoning the physical level and some passing to other levels of consciousness, as we have observed in subtle inner contact. The souls that reincarnate today seek to have their experiences in the most developed groups, and so the extinction of other groups became a tangible reality. And where do these souls go to? Will they enter into intra-terrestrial or supraphysical civilizations? Will they transmigrate to worlds that correspond to their present state of evolution?

In inner experience we have already encountered, in other planes of consciousness, representatives of these races in an advanced state of knowledge, ready to give us information for which we should be more prepared than we are. Are there on Earth human races that for us are still unknown because they are not on the concrete physical plane?

THE SECRET DOCTRINE hints to us about Divine Instructors for the present human Race: "Humanity and the stars are indissolubly united amongst themselves because of the intelligences that govern the latter."

Are there stellar intelligences amongst us?—we enquire silently. As we have seen, according to HPB, "our races are derived from divine races, whatever name we might give to the latter." But it is necessary to be careful when researching texts of ancient wise men, principally about temporal questions; today, for example "one uses the term century to designate one hundred years. In the times of Plato 100 thousand years signified one millennium. Therefore, for a time of 9 thousand years, the Initiates of today read 900 thousand", says HPB. This may be one of the reasons for divergences among scholars about the age of the Earth and of the humanity of the surface.

And what about those *born by themselves*, an expression which applies to all the Gods and Beings born from the will of a Divinity, or an Adept[11]? This may explain why we do not know the origin of the Count of Saint Germain, or why history has no account of when and how he disappeared. Nevertheless, he was well known in Europe, because he appeared and acted on the physical plane and, from 1710 to 1822, he appeared in several places. He was called Count of Saint Germain in France; Wonderman in Germany; Count Bellamore, in Venice; Prince Rakoczy, in Dresden.

---

11 An Adept is the one who, due to spiritual development, has reached transcending knowledge and powers, having arrived to the mastery of esoteric science. A Great Adept watches over the progress of humanity and directs it.

Faced with so many still unfathomable facts, HPB affirms that "some of the great Adepts will return in the Seventh Race, when all the mistakes will be undone and the advent of Truth will be proclaimed by those *Shishta*, as are called the sacred Sons of the Light."

Therefore, there is still much to learn here on this planet, and our union with peoples and civilizations that are not on the physical plane becomes a current question; and the opportunity to have new knowledge is being presented to trustworthy beings and groups. But this concept of *trustworthy*, according to HPB, includes that "the student of occultism must not belong to any specific creed or special sect; he must, however, show respect for all creeds and religions, if he aspires to become an Adept of the Good Law. He must be imprisoned neither by preconceptions nor by sectarian opinions, whatever they may be; he will have to form his convictions and arrive at his own conclusions, making use of the rules and methods of verification provided to him by the esoteric science, the study of which he has consecrated himself to. In this way, if the occultist, for example, follows Buddhism and considers Gautama Buddha to be the greatest Adept who ever existed, as the incarnation of Love free of egoism, of infinite charity and very pure moral, he will also see Jesus under the same beam of light, proclaiming him another incarnation of the divine virtues."

There are bold indications that HPB has made about the future. With time, according to her, "there will be more and more ether in the air; and when ether fills the air, then the creatures will be born without need of parents. In Virginia there is a special variety of plant that, without flowers, produces seedless fruit. A similar form of generation in the future will be extended, gradually, first to animals and later to the human species. Women will bear children without previous fertilization and in the Seventh Round[12] humans capable of self-reproducing will appear. People will become more psychic and, later, spiritual. Finally, they will be born *Buddhas* without sin."

Now let us transcribe some references from THE SECRET DOCTRINE about the new races:

"The occult philosophy teaches that, even now, under our own eyes, the new race and the future ones are in the process of formation, and that this transformation should occur in America, where it has silently already begun." One notices, however, that

---
12 Rounds are countless periods of time in which globes or worlds and "human principles" in an ascending order are developed.

this refers to immeasurable periods of time, that are impossible for the human mind to calculate.

"The Sixth Race will appear on the scene of our Round after cataclysms which, in their first phase, will one day destroy Europe, and later, all of the present Aryan race (thus reaching the two American continents) as well as most of the land adjoining the extreme boundaries of our continents and islands. When will this take place? Only the Great Masters of Wisdom know it; and they remain as silent as the snowy peaks that are in front of them.

"All that is known is that the Sixth Race will begin silently, so much in silence in fact, that during millenniums of years its pioneers—special children who will become special men and women—will be considered anomalous *lusus naturae*, abnormal rarities, physically and mentally. As they grow in number with the passing of time, there will arrive a day when they will be the majority. Then the humans of our time will be considered exceptional, until finally disappearing from the civilized countries, surviving only in small groups of islands—the mountain peaks of today—where they will vegetate and degenerate, to become extinct later…"

HPB continues:

"This process of preparation for the Sixth great Race will continue through the whole course of the sixth and seventh sub-races of the present Fifth Race[13]; but the last remainders of the Fifth Continent will only disappear some time after the birth of the new race: when a new dwelling place, the Sixth Continent, emerges on the waters on the surface of the globe to receive the new guest… In this way, the humanity of the New World has as mission and karma to plant the seeds of a future race, greater and much more glorious than all that we have known until now. The cycles of matter will be followed by cycles of spirituality and of complete mental development. According to the law of analogy of History and of the Races, most of future humanity will consist of glorious Adepts."

---

13 Each Root-Race—and they are seven—is composed of seven sub-races.

A life of contacts

HPB had contact with Adepts of several races, according to her biographers. Thus she was exposed to auras magnetized by energies of ascension. She traveled through the north and south of India, lived in Tibet, travelled through Persia, China and Egypt, certainly contacting the etheric and supraphysical levels of these regions that are anchor points of the universal energy on the planet. It is known that tourism, even spiritual tourism, has devitalized or contaminated the physical part of these regions; however, the supraphysical and invisible part maintains itself as a strategic point for the basic balance of the planet.

As regards the European nations, in some of them HPB also recognized the existence of adepts: in Greece, Hungary, Italy and England. In South America, according to her, in the inner levels there is a Lodge of Adepts—which we recognize in Ibez, at *Serra do Roncador*, Central Brazil.

HPB says: "The race of Adepts has a common origin with the ancient Egyptians, and Adepts are still preserving in inviolable secrecy the place where they live. There are certain members of the Lodges who go from center to center, keeping permanent lines of contact between them."

A journalist once asked her if Adepts communicated by means of astral bodies, as they are so physically distant one from the others. "Yes", she responded. "And in other still more elevated ways. They have in common their lives and their powers. As they elevate themselves spiritually, they place themselves above the differences in race, and for them there is only one humanity common to all. Their series is uninterrupted. Adepts are a necessity in Nature and Super-nature. They are links between humanity and the gods; and the word *gods* refers to the souls of great Adepts and Masters of previous races and ages, and so on as far as the threshold of Nirvana[14]. The continuity is uninterrupted."

"And what do they do?" inquired the journalist.

---
14 Nirvana is a state of absolute existence and consciousness that one who achieves a high degree of perfection and holiness enters during their lifetime.

"You would hardly understand it, unless you were an Adept. But they sustain and keep active the spiritual life of humanity."

"And how do they guide the souls of humanity?"

"In many ways, but principally through teaching their souls directly in the spiritual world. It is hard to understand this, but it is comprehensible. At certain regular intervals they try to transmit to the whole world a correct knowledge of spiritual things. They have records of the lives of all the Initiates. But this is not the only work of the Adepts. For much briefer periods of time they send a messenger to try to transmit teachings to the world."

All this, as we can see, is not part of the official history of the planet. But according to an observer, "history will crumble to the ground and will be reduced to dust during the XXth century, gnawed to the bone by those who write the annals." This is the harsh, predicted truth, as we can observe to date.

But there are other kinds of historians that we call spiritual researchers, who are always searching in planes of consciousness still mysterious or unknown to the great majority. HPB says: "Quite soon, in truth, by the combined effort of these *historians*, we will share the destiny of the cities lying in ruins in the two Americas, that are deeply covered by inaccessible virgin forest. These historical facts will remain hidden from view by the impenetrable jungle of the modern hypotheses of negativism and of skepticism. But fortunately, the *real* History always repeats itself, since it happens in cycles, and buried facts and occurrences deliberately sunk in the sea of skepticism of our days will emerge and reappear once again."

"All the ancient subterranean libraries and the vast treasures which must remain hidden until karma allows their return to human use are protected from the profane by the illusory perception of solid rocks, of a very hard soil, of a frightening abyss or by some other kind of obstacles."

In a more subtle observation, and always seeking the Light of the soul within those who search, HPB says that "one may describe the evolution of humanity by starting with those who are considered supernatural beings—Spirits—, which provokes criticism."

In the summary of Volume II of THE SECRET DOCTRINE[15], it says that "the esoteric history (which is

---
15 THE SECRET DOCTRINE—The Synthesis of Science, Religion and Philosophy, Volume II, by Helena P. Blavatsky. Theosophical Publishing House, Wheaton, IL. 1993.

different from the official history) is veiled by symbols. The language of mystery today is called symbolism. The religious and esoteric history of each people was embedded in symbols; it was never literally expressed in many words. All the feelings and emotions, all the knowledge and teachings acquired by the first races or revealed to them, found their pictorial expression in allegory and in parable."

And still: "There is a system transmitted to humanity by beings of a more advanced race, so elevated that they appeared to be *divine* to the eyes of that childish humanity; in a word, by beings originating from other spheres."

It was Koot Hoomi, today Khutullim and second hierarchy in Miz Tli Tlan, who wrote to HPB:

"Knowledge can only be communicated gradually; and some of the most elevated secrets if exposed would seem without meaning. Occult science is not something whose secrets can be disclosed all of a sudden, by writings or even by verbal communication. (...) The truth is: until the neophyte attains the condition of reaching a certain degree of enlightenment, many secrets, if not all, will remain incommunicable. The receptivity of the being must equal the desire for instruction. Enlightenment must come from within."

HPB added that first "it is necessary to transmute the lower animal nature of the human being into what is more elevated and divine. It is a matter of combining the masculine and the feminine principle, what the East calls the harmonization of *yin* and of *yang*; and this alchemy is done through silent work and self-sacrifice."

Finally, "it is a matter of perfect harmonization of the divine with the human in humanity, the adjustment of its qualities and divine aspirations and the control over the terrestrial and animal passions. And, if the individual seeks spirituality, he or she does not need formal religion."

A poet says that waves advance through our deepest being, elevating us without our awareness, and freeing us from minor questions. Let us be conscious of this inner and major work, and carry out our part with the necessary Love for the Evolutionary Plan and for Creation.

"A Sole and Universal Divinity is a principle, a fundamental and abstract idea. It is not a question of a personal and anthropomorphic God, which is nothing but a vision of humanity, according to its perspective. It is about a divine universal Principle, source of *everything*, from which everything proceeds and in which everything will be absorbed at the end of the great evolutionary cycle. It is absolute and infinite, it is everywhere, from the atom to the Cosmos, both visible and invisible. It is the mysterious power of evolution and of involution, the creative potentiality, omnipresent, omnipotent and omniscient. It is absolute thought and absolute existence", says the Glossary that HPB left to humanity.[16]

"There are inferior deities which are transitory personifications of the sky, the stars, the elements, the forces or phenomena of Nature, and for all these, humans have different names. But the One is unnamable."

"There are planetary Spirits[17] whose collective aggregate forms the manifest Verb of the un-manifest Logos; there are advanced devas (corresponding to the Archangels of religions), some related to the Sun. They represent the light, the day, just as those related to darkness represent the night."

---

16 THE THEOSOPHICAL GLOSSARY, by Helena P. Blavatsky. Theosophical Publishing House, Wheaton, IL.
17 Also called planetary Gods. At first they were the regents and governors of the planets. The Earth has its hierarchy of terrestrial planetary spirits, from the most elevated plane to the lowest one, as any other heavenly body has. However, in occultism the term is applied only to the highest Hierarchies, corresponding to the Archangels.

"The divine and supreme Self of humanity is called the inner God. It is a particle of the Universal Spirit within us, which dwells in our hearts. It is called the individual Spirit, and the external self, or personality of humans, can contact this level, but only if the search becomes their priority in life."

"This God within humanity is in the deep silence of the Being, beyond all appearances. Concentrating the mind to some inner point, and abstracting yourself from everything pertaining to the external universe and that of the senses, humans come to perceive it."

"When they have ceased listening to the many, humans will be able to discern the ONE", declares THE VOICE OF THE SILENCE. "Only then, and not before, will he or she abandon the region of the false to enter the realm of truth."

And, she continues:

"Fight with your impure thoughts before they dominate you. Deal with them as they want to treat you, because if spared, they will grow roots and expand and—notice it well—these thoughts will dominate you and kill you."

"Do not desire anything. Do not struggle against karma or against the unchangeable laws of Nature. But fight only with what is personal, transitory and perishable."

"Help Nature and cooperate with it, and Nature will view you as one of its creators and will become obedient. And before you it will open the portals of its secret chambers, and will disclose before your view the treasures hidden in the depth of its pure, virginal womb."

The cosmic spirituality

The cosmic attraction, also called the Cosmic Magnet, stimulates the spirit infinitely. The Cosmos operates by attraction, and its basic principle is Hierarchy. Therefore, each movement of the Hierarchy manifests the cosmic qualities, and we are attracted to a central nucleus of perfect harmony.

The Universe is full of harmony, and Harmony is a supreme pattern. When persons withdraw from this principle their difficulties begin. And, when they separate themselves from the principle of Hierarchy, they disorganize themselves.

Hierarchy and Harmony synthesize cosmic spirituality. Without harmony we become unstable, unable to communicate with the Highest. Ordinary consciousness has no interest in this communication, essential for a creative and healthy life.

In our attempts in the direction of this contact with the the Most High, the results seem imperceptible. This occurs because the actions of the superior energies do not seem evident to us. But only the simple fact that we are trying such Communication brings to us infinite joy and fearlessness. And without fear, one comes closer to the Light.

Light is understanding, higher understanding.

Light has been assured for humanity, but humanity almost always does not accept it. And the Cosmos increases this Light until the infinite, as well as its offer to humanity. Without Light we do not have access to the more subtle currents of life, closer to the center of cosmic spirituality.

Light is necessary for recognizing the invisible forces, more potent than the visible ones. The New is still invisible to this humanity, and there is urgency to perceive it. If we do not begin to perceive the distant worlds, for example, and if the inner worlds are not within our reach, we will not be able to comprehend anything of the Cosmos, here on the plane of forms. Remaining restricted to the terrestrial consciousness, we do not receive redeeming energy that attracts us to other planes of consciousness, beyond the planetary limits. On this path we are moving slowly when could already be trained as consciousnesses to live new forces and energies. Inner worlds and distant worlds can be perceived quite clearly, but we would have to dedicate ourselves to the observation of our interior, and through that arrive to the interior of the Universe, where we will find the greatest synthesis that we need.

This is the path that will change our ordinary existence.

One of the reasons why the Earth is ailing is due to the fact that the light and the energetic rays of certain planets cannot enter its aura. "What will humanity be reduced to", asks Morya, a Master of the great Yoga, "if it ceases to commune with the higher consciousness and plunges into vulgar ignorance? Losing the comprehension of the higher worlds, people get far from the awareness of improvement."

The structure of the State and the organized religions do not lead people to this vision. On the contrary, the supernatural is continuously replaced by what is most concrete, removing the beauty and scope of spiritual life, which should be a day to day practice.

But, even so, a new consciousness grows—which, despite being still inexperienced, challenges and keeps on dissolving the old thoughts. Those who still lean on people and mental forms of the past will find themselves in situations without an exit; and their subtle bodies, during sleep or in moments of inner contact, cannot experiment with taking off into space or plunging into the inner consciousness of the planets.

Through the centuries we have accumulated habits and customs which have densified our thoughts. And even physical modifications will be necessary to make alterations in stratified concepts existing in humanity. It will be necessary to make drastic changes in our physical life and still more drastic changes in the physical reality of the surface of the planet.

Our inner contacts are impaired by unstable moods and weak concentration. Personal interests predominate, and not everyone creates the time necessary for communication with the inner planes of life and of our own selves.

The search for direct knowledge, which will lead to greater spirituality, requires aspiration to reach it and to make this goal a priority. Without the higher spirituality as our goal little can be achieved on the ascending path. We know that only the best and the most simple are those who have dedicated themselves to cultivate such aspiration. But those who live in the average human consciousness, without uneasiness, end up being taken over by their prejudices, and the routine of daily and conventional life kills the delicate impulses of the soul and spirit.

An important key within spirituality is to dedicate not only our idle time to the search for attunement with the Most High, but to really pervade all of our life with this aspiration.

A little yoga story tells us about what a dark spirit thought: "How may I tie more firmly humanity to Earth? Let them keep their usual habits and customs. Nothing is as binding to humanity as ordinary images." And, for this, the dark forces labor tirelessly.

But where should we direct our will, which is something so powerful and unknown to most people, and where should the thoughts and aspiration be placed? At the same time that we focus on our inner part we should learn to head towards the infinite space, towards superior worlds and towards beings who have already passed beyond our present stage and await the slightest sign to attune with us and instruct us on matters of the Universe.

In Volume II of THE SECRET DOCTRINE a law of occult universal dynamics is revealed: "An amount of energy developed on the spiritual plane produces much greater effects than the same amount applied on the physical plane of objective existence."

And everything indicates that it is possible for human beings to function on this plane.

The theosophical knowledge for the Future Race

To affirm the future one needs the energy of the warrior. And, while one affirms the future, one increases the power to build it. It is necessary to be in this attunement, as obstacles will arise in proportion to one's aspiration, because it also attracts particles of will that oppose it. It is said about this that: "when a ship increases its speed, the force of resistance of the waves increases." However, we know that it is by keeping the focus in the heart lit that a person is prevented from succumbing to the burden of circumstances. "Try the ocean. The big waves will give happiness to you," say the yogi's codes.

When one considers learning about the methods of the Future Race, one must know that each period brings its own. The Instructors say that seeking solutions in old methods "is like trying to wear your grandfather's boots"—which does not signify despising what the past has given us—nor that one does not have to make an important synthesis incorporating data from the past, if correctly considered.

There are certain keys to prepare us as a future race:

1. Eliminate fear, which hinders the correct attitude during an action.

2. Cultivate silence, which is the appropriate atmosphere to maintain in the inner world.

3. Discern the quality and quantity of one's own load, and throw off what is useless.

4. Promise nothing to anyone.

5. Possess few things, only the necessary ones.

6. Never sell the Teachings as they are for the common good.

7. Eradicate cunning, which is synonymous with deference, and cultivate ingenuity, which is a devotional movement.

8. Never expect to be rewarded.

9. Know that the highest experience is that about oneself, that of the donation of one's own spirit in benefit of humanity.

10. Have your own intellect only as an instrument for reasoning, knowing that the direct knowledge is in the wisdom of the higher self, which is SYNTHESIS.

Abandoning one's own memories one begins to search for the consciousness of the New Earth with more freedom. One begins to find then a principle of unity; one sees the old world in all the continents, and the new world being born everywhere, independently of the conditions existing in the countries and beyond all and any border. The New World differs from the Old World in consciousness and not in appearance. Age, circumstances, nationality, all this loses its importance.

And, as we have seen, but which is for us to repeat, the control of fear is a true threshold for the new consciousness. Those who aspire to the future abandon all and every trace of the past in their temperament, due to recognizing the overload that it represents. And fear had its origin in the remote past of humanity and accompanies it until today.

All true group action diminishes fear and is equivalent to an increase in strength; and groups of 12 people, if truly united can determine great events. But one should not be anxious to enlarge the groups, because an expansion could make them weaker by altering the dynamics of their formation. If differences in karmic conditions begin to enter the group, these could change the circumstances of work in the group and decrease their efficiency. We must avoid, in well-formed groups, undesired presences, and primarily, all the members should try to settle old debts in their own lives, to simplify karma.

Good intentions without explicit action limit a person and prevent contact with the energetic currents that may already be emanated by the distant and inner worlds. We know that only sometime in the future the energy of the distant worlds will reach our material bodies, but it is necessary that we prepare ourselves to begin to receive it. And this is indispensable for us to have a truly new and adequate action.

Groups that are well consolidated give to each collaborator the elements necessary not to waste forces to be used for the work of the Plan, and not to be so busy with physical necessities. Objects without immediate use to a certain member should be placed at the disposal of the group, but always avoiding, obviously, mixing of auras and vibrations.

In the future races, people will never consider having specialization. A being specialized in something is suitable only for the conditions of this Earth—which will bring about reincarnations. The Spirit deals with other spheres; it deals with the expansion of the soul energy, which opens the path to the invisible.

Although in many cases technological improvement is necessary, the essential thing is to refine thought. This is what will influence multitudes of consciousnesses. The Masters say that "each conscious thought seeks the future course of evolution" and that "the Teaching does not force the approach but indicates the way to reach it."

"It is necessary to be deeply aware of the future. The work does not finish with predestined tasks, but continues infinitely. The revelation of the Infinite is the most beautiful aspiration", we are told very clearly.

As we can see from these texts, the Instructors of HPB were always precise and when they published instructions such as these so that everyone could know them, they wrote that it is "the solitude of the Spirit that produces the idea of future forms."

But who is really in search of solitude—which does not mean separateness or exclude being in group but which includes acting in community?

The next race will be characterized by spiritual development, by acquisition of the sixth sense, that is, astral clairvoyance, and by humanitarian tendencies. It will populate the continent *Zaha*, whose emersion will occur where North America is today, which will have been destroyed by earthquakes and by volcanic fires, according to HPB.

At this point we must remember that, when speaking of future times, we are placing ourselves in the *real* time, which is not the material one, the time of clocks, but the result of a great transformation in the mind of human beings: when they begin to succeed in conceiving an *eternal present*, without past or future.

As for the last race, it will be characterized by complete spiritual development, by the acquisition of the seventh sense, that is mental clairvoyance, and by the full recognition of unity. It will flourish on the seventh continent called *Puchkara*, whose center will be in what we now call South America.

While in the mind of the human being all this takes place through the material time of clocks, one can suppose that the present human race (the Fifth) has existed for 1 million years, and that it has as main objective to develop the mind. Developing in seven sub-races, with 210 thousand years for each, it will still be flourishing for countless time. But if all this happens in our consciousness in the *eternal present*, then all the races are already existing—otherwise, no clairvoyant could see such an extensive picture.

Is this about learning to remain in the Present, the only real time?

Is there, in the present, someone who lives this as a pioneer? There seems to be.

New dharmic patterns after the planetary purification

Dharma is the Sacred Law but, according to HPB, it is also "the inner nature, characterized in each human by the degree of development that he or she has acquired." It is considered as well as "the law that determines the development in the evolutionary period that comes next." A broader understanding of the term dharma is "that which shapes external life through thoughts, words and actions."

But dharma is not something external, such as virtue, religion, justice or the regular law of the world. "It is the law of life which reveals itself and gives shape to everything that is external to it." The word dharma has been given many meanings, but it is our intention to accentuate only a few of them, so they can be deepened.

Behavior, therefore influences dharma, and at each moment many things can keep changing. If the mind is free, it will look for combinations, it will arrange patterns which will elevate matter to other levels. Animals, our younger brothers, are not conscious of the consequences of their actions; but humans, if they have the will to KNOW, will reach a less common comprehension and will feel with this deep joy. Acquiring this comprehension, if aspiration is kept elevated, dharma will lead to conscious cooperation with superior worlds, still distant to most human beings. So, according to dharma, humanity will feel more fortunate and more capable of weighing the consequences of its day-to-day actions.

Those who consider their own knowledge insignificant and who do not follow the common mind of people are in a favorable dharmic path. Having reached this point, they will not give importance to terrestrial heredity, and will renew themselves continually.

One of the great Instructors of HPB tells us in AGNI YOGA[18] that it is a matter of "smiling at the storm that swept away previous achievements; of losing the ability to slander; of intensifying the aspiration in search of the invisible Supreme; of not associating

---
18 AGNI YOGA, Agni Yoga Society. New York, USA. 1954.

with the traitors of truth." And still, we should, "be involved with *pure* thought, which forms an invincible aura."

In this dharma, we change the goal of our own work and we uplift our own knowledge. "Each conscious thought seeks the future course of evolution; and, if the direction is sensed, healthy reason will try to approximate itself to the correct path more quickly." But the Teaching does not force the approximation: it simply shows the way and leaves us free to accept it or not.

One must, however, have always present the concept of refinement. Refinement leads to spiritual growth. But self-refinement happens slowly and begins with intention and correct thought. Correct thought disciplines us and leads us to a greater evolution. And daily life, within this dharma, becomes rich and valuable.

Even the Teaching is to be constantly re-examined, to be amplified and updated, so that it is as close as possible to our actions. "The one who has no fear to see the light, has eagle eyes", say the Agni Yoga Teachings. "The one who has no fear to enter in the fire, is from fiery birth. The one who has no fear of the invisible, can cross darkness. When we lose something, we become free of passion." And, insisting, the Teachings repeat with new words: "Every action must be permeated by purifying, fiery aspiration."

Today, more than ever, an adequate discipline which does not attack others and which attracts little attention is necessary. It is a matter of having a discipline full of joy and sense of responsibility. With it we have open doors to greater steps. However, "beware of the ones who scattered the seeds of the world in their own garden—because joy is for the one who gave out each seed of comprehension to the Common Good." This is the call for all who have decided to serve the planet. This is a principle for living the Service within the Spiritual Law.

So extensive is the work on this planet, evolutionary work, that all the possible forces are necessary and must be gathered for this purpose. Everyone, without the exception of anyone, can be one of the builders of the coming future. There is work for everyone, in all the degrees of ability and quality of intention. Humanity finds enthusiasm and time for so much degrading work, but it is time to change this, and for humanity to dedicate itself to dignified work.

We all know that the plans for the New Earth and the New Humanity are pleasing almost exclusively to the simple souls. The Teachings point out that "on the eve of a catastrophe, we tried to lead the people to the outside of an amusement park. Not only did the people not leave, but the crowd still tried to get in."

This is the normal reality, and those who dedicate themselves to education, or who include themselves in the task of rescuing of souls are before it. But it is said, knowingly, that it is the solitary spirit that provides the future shape of life. Do not find it strange, therefore, if we find ourselves alone. And why do so many avoid the unusual, the unknown? Could it not be because they are encouraged in schools to live like the majority?

New forms of thought come with aspiration, with the aspiration from those who love the Unknown. "There is little hope for the multitudes, but the Rock of the distant star brings the solitary message", say the Instructors of HPB in Agni Yoga. The Masters and the Instructors have always created the future with the power of their thoughts, never based upon the conscience of the multitude.

❖ ❖ ❖

Humans must transcend the stage of applying what they know exclusively for their *own* future. Humanity still uses the benefits for *itself*, and in this way reduces the world to its own *self*. This limitation destroys most of the opportunities that life offers.

People are little conscious of world tasks and very rarely accomplish them with the participation of large groups. But it is unnecessary to be pessimistic in these times; rather, it is about launching our values to the future. Thus, we will be constructing from this moment on a new reality. Each moment lived, each step well-taken can be building from now on that which will exist after the general planetary purification. As the evolution of Humanity is inseparable from cosmic processes, according to a certain law, we must create a new understanding during this period of transition, no matter how dark it may seem to be.

After the night the dawn will finally appear, and in the new dawn we can be consciously living in all the bodies and with the forces of the soul.

Just as when constructing a new building one must demolish the old one, so when everything has collapsed to the ground the space will be free for the New Life. In this sense, we consider the present downfall of values as the foretelling of the new construction.

This comprehension of the perennial currents of Energy is for us the beginning of understanding the cosmic currents. But we have to aspire for this.

And the Instructors have shown us the difference between expectation and aspiration: "In expectation there is always a moment of inactivity, whereas in aspiration there is always a flight to the future. This difference can only be perceived by the one who is not satisfied with the course of present life and who thinks about the incessant course of existence in other planets"—of which one can in some way aspire to participate.

Small fragments of the Great Silence[19]

"Seek the Path. But cleanse your heart before you undertake your journey. Before the first step, learn to discern the real from the false, the permanent from the fleeting. Learn, above all, to separate mental erudition from the Wisdom of the soul."

"Even ignorance is preferable to mental erudition without the Wisdom of the soul to enlighten it and guide it. The mind is like a mirror: it gathers dust while it reflects. You must seek to fuse your mind into the soul."

"Prepare yourself because you will have to travel alone. The Instructor can only show the way. The Path is one for everyone; but the means to reach the

---
19 Phrases freely translated from THE VOICE OF THE SILENCE, by Helena P. Blavatsky. Theosophical Publishing House, IL., 1982.

Goal varies among pilgrims. The rough Path winds its way up the mountain. Three times great is the one who climbs the very high peak."

"You will have to open passages through fortresses guarded by cruel and cunning powers—the incarnate passions. Do not allow the senses to become the playing field of the mind."

"There are many Instructors; but the Master-Soul (Universal Soul) is only one. Live in this Master, as His ray lives in you. Live in your fellow being, as your fellow being lives in Him."

"The Portals to Knowledge and Wisdom are seven:

1. Charity and immortal love.

2. Harmony in words and actions (gets rid of the balancing karmic action).

3. Sweet patience that nothing can disturb.

4. Indifference to pleasure and to pain, transcendence of illusion, perception of reality.

5. Daring energy that opens the path from lie to the Supreme Truth.

6. Incessant contemplation.

7. Perception."

"Learn that no effort, however small—both in the right direction and in the wrong direction—can vanish from the world of causes. Even dispersed smoke leaves traces. Any word brusquely uttered in past lives will not be lost, but is always reborn. The pepper tree will not bear roses, neither will the silvery star of the jasmine become a thorn or thistle."

"Today you can create tomorrow's opportunities. Along the Great Journey, the causes that are sown in each moment will produce the corresponding harvest of effects."

"It is from the bud of renunciation of the little self that is born the sweet fruit of final Liberation. The pilgrim who wants to cool his limbs in running water, but does not dare to plunge into it because of dread of the currents, risks perishing from the heat."

"Inaction based on selfish fear will give nothing but bad fruits. The person who does not accomplish the task that he or she was assigned in life, lives in vain."

"Follow the wheel of duty towards race and family, friend and foe, and immunize your mind to pleasure and pain."

"Have you attuned your being to the great pain of humanity, O seeker of Light?"

"Living for the benefit of humanity is the first step. The second one is practicing the six glorious virtues: charity, morality, patience, energy, contemplation, wisdom. Reaching the bliss of Nirvana and renouncing it is the final, supreme step—the highest in the Path of Renunciation."

"The last ones will be the greatest. The Master of Perfection renounced his Self to save the world, detaining himself at the threshold of the immaculate state."

"Sweet are the fruits of Repose and of Liberation for love of the Self; however, sweeter still are the fruit of long and arduous duty: the Renouncing for love of others, for the fellow beings that are suffering."

"Do not trust in the senses. Avoid compliments. Compliments lead to self-illusion. Turn your face away from the deceptions of the world."

"Devotion can restore to you the knowledge that was yours in previous births."

"Give light and comfort to the tired pilgrim. Seek the one who knows less than you do, that one who in his miserable desolation is famished for the bread of wisdom, that one who is without Instructor, hope or consolation. Lead him to hear the Law."

"Perfection can seem remote, very remote; but the pilgrim has taken the first step. He has entered in the current and may acquire the sight of the mountain eagle, the hearing of the shy doe."

"If you cannot be the Sun, then be the humble planet. Although without distinction and lost among many others, it shows the Path, as the evening star does for those who follow its trail in the dark."

"Be more humble, once you have acquired Wisdom. Be more humble still when you have mastered Wisdom. Be like the ocean that receives all the rivers and streams. Its immense serenity remains unaltered; it does not feel them."

"Presumption resembles a high tower in which an arrogant lunatic has climbed. The arrogant person proudly repeats: 'Look, I know.' The humble confess in a lowered voice: 'I heard it like this'."

"True knowledge is the flour, false erudition is the husk."

"The lamp shines when wick and oil are clean. The flame does not feel the cleansing process."

"It is necessary to reach self-knowledge; self-knowledge is the child of loving action."

"Persevere as one who has to persist eternally."

"Accept the pains of birth."

"Walk away from the sunlight into the shade in order to open space for others."

"Be watchful of what is inferior so it will not blemish that which is Superior."

"Before you are established in the Path of Knowledge and call it yours, and if you want to conquer good and evil, your soul must become like the fruit of the mango tree: tender and sweet like its golden pulp for the pains and anxieties of others, and hard as its pit for your own pains and anxieties."

"Strengthen your soul against the tricks of the self; make it deserve the name of *Diamond Soul*. Just as a diamond buried deep in the beating heart of the Earth never reflects the lights from the surface, so the soul and the mind immersed in the path of knowledge must reflect nothing from the realm of illusion."

"Guard against inconstancy, because it is your great enemy. If it prevails it will drive you away from the Path and hurl you to the bottom of the swamps of doubt. Prepare yourself and protect yourself in time. If you have tried to persevere and have failed, do not lose courage; keep up the battle and renew the charge repeatedly."

"Remember, you who fight for the liberation of humanity: each failure is a success, and each sincere attempt gains its reward at the right time. Blessed seeds sprout and grow invisibly in the soul of the disciple. Their stems grow stronger at each new trial. They bend like rushes, but do not break, or could ever be wasted. When the hour sounds, they will bloom."

"If you came prepared, fear nothing. Fear destroys the will and paralyzes all action."

"Stand firm. Bathe the soul in the essence of Patience. Do not be frightened. The habit of fear rusts the key, and a rusty key will refuse to open the lock. The more you progress, the more traps your feet will meet."

"The Path of progress is lightened by a single flame: the daring, burning in the heart. The more you dare, the more you gain. If you fear, the light dims—and only it can guide you."

"Prepare yourself for the portal of temptations that binds the inner man. If you long to triumph on the Path of virtue, you will need, more than ever, to have the mind and perceptions free from mortal deeds."

"If you want the Wisdom of celestial origin, painfully gained, to flow like sweet running waters, you must not let it turn into a stagnant pond. You must spread the light acquired through all the range of the three worlds: terrestrial, astral and spiritual. The torrent of super-human knowledge that you have reached must be poured by you into other channels. These waters, pure and cool, must be used to sweeten the bitter waves of the immense sea of suffering formed from the tears of humans. Give light to all but never take it from anyone."

"Become like the white snow in the valleys of the mountains, cold and insensitive to touch, warm and protecting to the seed which sleeps deep under its cloak. It is this snow which must receive the biting frost, the winds of the north, thus protecting from its sharp teeth the earth which guards the promised harvest, which will give bread to those who are hungry."

"Calm and impassive the pilgrim glides. He knows that the more his feet bleed, the more he will become clean and white."

"The Divine Compassion is the LAW of laws—everlasting Harmony, universal essence, light of eternal Justice, balance of all things, perpetual love. The more you unite to this law, the more your being blends with it, the more your soul unites with that which is, the more you will become absolute compassion."

"Now bow your head and listen well. Says the Divine Compassion: 'Can there be bliss while all that lives must suffer? Do you want to save yourself while hearing the entire world crying?'"

"Now you know—choose your path."

❖ ❖ ❖

"You have to be filled with the pure Universal Soul, make yourself one with the Thought-Soul of Nature. United with it, you are invincible; separated you transform yourself into the playground of relative truth, origin of all the illusions of the world."

"Everything is transitory in humans, except for the pure and brilliant essence of the Universal Soul."

"A much more difficult task awaits you: you have to feel yourself totally as thought and, nevertheless, banish from your soul all thoughts."

"You have to achieve that fixed mind in which no breeze or wind, however strong, can place an earthly thought within it. Thus purified, your Sanctuary should be completely empty of worldly action, sound or light."

"Thus it is written in the BHAGAVAD-GITA: 'Before the golden white flame can burn and illuminate with stability a light, the lamp must remain well protected where it can be hidden safely from all breezes. Exposed to the changing breeze, the beam of light flickers and the faltering flame casts into the white shrine of the soul deceitful, dark, and trembling shadows.'"

And the instructors of HPB continue:

"Govern your thoughts, if you want to safely cross the threshold of perfection."

"Govern your soul, if you want to reach the Goal. Fix the eye of your soul on the One, Pure Light, Light free from attachments, and use your Key of Gold."

"Your labor, a tiring task, is almost done. You are ready to cross the broad chasm open wide to swallow you up."

"You have already crossed over the ditch that surrounds the gate of human passions. You have expelled the stains and impure desires from your heart. But your task is still not finished. Build a high wall to enclose your higher ego, your thinking self; raise the barrier that will protect you from the proud satisfaction of accomplishing a great deed."

"A feeling of vanity would blemish the work. Yes, build a strong barrier, so that you will not be swallowed up at the very moment of achieving victory."

ADDITIONAL POINTS

Invisible worlds

"There are millions and millions of worlds that we can see; but much greater is the number of those that are beyond the reach of telescopes, and a great many of them do not belong to our objective plane of existence. Although as invisible as if they were situated at an immeasurable distance from our Solar System, they coexist with us, near us, within our own world, and are as objective and material to their respective inhabitants as our world is to us. But the relationship between these worlds and ours is not like that of the series of oval boxes contained one inside the other, in the style of certain Chinese toys; each world is subject to its own laws and special conditions, without having direct relationship with our sphere.

The inhabitants of these worlds, as we have already said, can, without our knowing or feeling it—

be passing *through us* or *at our sides*, as in an open space; their dwelling places interpenetrate with ours without disturbance to our vision, because we still do not have the faculties necessary for their perception. However, thanks to their spiritual sight, the Adepts and even certain clairvoyants and sensitives can distinguish, in a greater or lesser degree, their presence among us and the proximity of beings who belong to other spheres of life. Those who live in the spiritually superior worlds only communicate with terrestrial mortals who, by their individual efforts, elevate themselves to the higher plane they occupy (...).

It is not a question of superstition, but simply of transcendent science; it is still more a question of logic, to admit the existence of worlds made of matter that is much more tenuous than the tail of a comet."

THE SECRET DOCTRINE
VOLUME II

The new Ten Commandments

There is an etheric replica, an *akashic* register of the Tablets of Moses in Mount Sinai.

The physical tablets, the stones, exist but are protected. At some moments they were taken outside the planet, but today they are in the Intraterrestrial Retreats.

Shamballa and Miz Tli Tlan[20] have direct relation with the tablets and with their protection. And Mount Sinai is an entrance to Shamballa.

The Hierarchies have the intention to reveal the Ten Commandments, amplified and explained, which will serve as a guide for the new planetary era.

---

20 Shamballa was the most powerful planetary center active in the cycle that ended on 8/8/88. Miz Tli Tlan is the planetary center that currently rules the others.

Initially the Ten Commandments were the ten guidelines that human beings must comply with so that the genetic project could be carried out. The Ten Commandments have a spiritual aspect which remains in the Universe, but which is not respected. Human beings understood them from the concrete point of view, but their reality is deeper.

They were a channelization by the one who we know today in the inner levels of life as Joaquel, who was known at that time as Moses. He received them during the biblical exodus and had to introduce this energy to all those consciousnesses because all of them should be developing tasks of the Evolutionary Plan today.

Most of those who were in the desert are incarnated today.

The contact with the Serpent, which they recognized as a serpent of gold of EXODUS, tried to imprint the spiritual contact with Enoch, an aspect of Emmanuel, an aspect of the One and Only God. Moses had as his task to manifest this information, this symbol, so it could be understood as an answer from God. But the people took it as a symbol to worship.

In that time what was tried was to introduce to people a mental cosmic energy, an aspect of Enoch. But the history written by humans and the BIBLE tell another story, and confusion arose from this.

Jerusalem guards the archetype of the DIVINE CITY, a city organized in the points and patterns of the Laws of Emmanuel. We have always attempted to shape it, but the human substance could not stand the incarnation of these patterns. This archetype must be recovered and translated, because it contains the energy of a new civilization.

There are other etheric cities like Jerusalem. And according to communications from Saint Germain to a well-known esoteric society about the main deserts, they exist. However, 144 incarnate beings must embody the Holy Spirit, and the manifestation of the Holy Spirit through them will open a portal for the reentry of the materialized Christ on the planet.

Humanity should know, and should be made to understand, that many, many times the inhabitants of cities go through what is called death and reincarnate in the same place because they have made connections which attract them once again to the same environments. However, the disciple who must reincarnate for service must take up the command:

"The next time I will be born into a family of great Light." This will allow a very quick progress.

(Transmitted to the contact group on 3/23/2009)

Karma

HPB says, in Volume II of The Secret Doctrine:

"It is not karma that punishes or rewards, but it is us who reward or punish ourselves, according to how we work with Nature, for Nature and in accordance with Nature, obeying the laws upon which this Harmony depends or transgressing them."

"The ways of karma are not impenetrable if humans allow union and harmony to govern their actions instead of orienting them according to disunity and conflict…"

"If not one man harmed his fellow being, karma would have no reason to intervene, or weapons with which to execute its task. It is the constant presence among us of the elements of struggle and of opposition, it is in the division of races, nations, tribes, societies and individuals into Cains and Abels, wolves and lambs, which constitute the main cause for what is called the Paths of Providence. With our own hands we set daily the winding course of our destinies, believing we are following in a straight line along the real path of respectability and duty—and we complain later that they are so gloomy and inextricable, these winding curves..."

"In truth, there is no accident in our lives, there is no bad day or misfortune whose cause cannot be found in our own actions, in this or another existence. If persons infringe the laws of harmony or, according to the expression used by a theosophist, the 'laws of life', they must be prepared to fall into the chaos that they themselves produced."

"The One Life is intimately related to the One Law that governs the world of the being: karma."

"In its exoteric and literal sense, karma means action, a cause that produces effects. But esoterically it is something different in its far reaching moral effects. It is the infallible LAW OF RETRIBUTION."

Dreams, portals to the inner world

We dream during the whole night, but little do we remember of what happens while the physical body sleeps. The activity of the astral and mental bodies when they are separated from the physical body during its sleep is something that we could control, or at least, follow consciously.

HPB suggests that "we ask for dreams that can be imprinted in memory by the higher self, because these are simple and clear. They do not consist of visions or of vague situations, caught by the brain and distorted by fantasy, as is normal."

"The higher self can imprint even events pertaining to past incarnations, and these dreams are genuine and clarify the origins of certain conditions in the present. We can ask the higher self to avoid having allegoric dreams, that is, vague visions of realities captured by the brain, as we have referred to above. These are only partly true as indications, and we must remain neutral towards them and without any anxiety so that they do not influence us."

HPB was asked whether there were ways to interpret dreams. "Only by means of the clairvoyance and the spiritual intuition of the interpreter. Each ego that dreams is different from all the others, in the same way as are our physical bodies."

"Generally", says HPB, "we can divide dreams into seven types:

1. Prophetic dreams. They are imprinted in our memory by the higher self and are generally simple and clear. Or a voice is heard or an upcoming event is seen beforehand.

2. Allegoric dreams or vague visions of realities captured by the brain and distorted by our fantasies. They are only in part true. They show the connection we may have in certain matters.

3. Dreams sent by Adepts[21]—good or bad adepts—by mesmerizers or by thoughts of very

---
21 Beings who protect the development of humanity, when positive. See note on page 38 for more information

powerful minds that want us to obey their wishes.

4. Retrospective dreams of events pertaining to past incarnations. They can be memories from a deeper level.

5. Warning dreams for other people who are unable to receive the information directly. Regarding these, it is necessary to have discernment about sharing them, because sometimes they come to provide us with cues to deal adequately with someone.

6. Confused dreams, which have causes that have already been explained above. They are mixtures of stimuli or elements captured from collective levels.

7. Dreams that are mere fantasies and chaotic images, due to bad digestion, to some mental problems or some external cause."

THE SECRET DOCTRINE, in Volume III[22] affirms that "there are seven keys of interpretation for each symbol or allegory. The meaning that may not satisfy, for example, the psychological or astronomical aspect

---

[22] THE SECRET DOCTRINE—The Synthesis of Science, Religion and Philosophy, Volume III, by Helena P. Blavatsky, Theosophical Publishing House, Wheaton, IL 1993

will be, nevertheless, completely correct from a physical or metaphysical point of view."

HPB searched for the unknown and, in this way, found her inner Instructor in dreams. And, in dreams, He instructed her.

> (Adapted from a study by HPB to be found in the Minutes of Blavatsky Lodge of the Theosophical Society)

CONCLUDING TOPICS

An addition to the texts of Blavatsky

It is part of the plan for these times that an opening in human consciousness will occur on a large scale as a last phase of expansion before the final moments of the stage of purification of the Earth.

In this cycle the conscious and guided expansion will start and where there is openness the process will begin or continue. Three distinct phases can be observed:

FIRST PHASE: The opening of the being will permit one of three degrees of expansion: 1, 2 or 3.

Degree One: See apparent realities, have perceptions in the etheric level, such as the evident auric subtle field, and surrounding energies.

Degree Two: Have extra-sensorial perception of an ad-vanced character and to have the sense organs available in other dimensions.

Degree Three: Have cosmic extraterrestrial perception, of an inner nature, that is, that which the inner being permits to be captured from the Cosmos and to arrive to the terrestrial mind.

SECOND PHASE: Active participation of the being in the integration between basic inferior levels. Improvement of telepathic and extra-systemic contact (contact between planets from different solar systems).

THIRD PHASE: Conscious action of the being in the cosmic level. The mind that reaches this level is immersed in cosmic fluid that comes from linked civilizations which have accompanied the being since the beginning. The expansion after this phase enables the being to merge with the Purpose and become one with it.

The first phase is available to everyone and has already begun.

The second phase is for those who persist in TRUTH. Illusion and lies hinder the pilgrim's progress.

This is a broad phase and it demands care in order to avoid producing wrong interpretations.

The third phase is for disciples who did not give up when faced with trials and who have awakened to Reality with awareness of communion, fidelity and reverence to the Plan that guides them.

Everything depends on surrender, on love and on the degree of aspiration of the seeker.

The doors are open.

Seven paths open to the advanced human being

1. "As soon as the human kingdom is crossed, humans reach the threshold of super-human life and then become free spirits. Before them, seven paths open for their choice:

2. Blessed omniscience and omnipotence on the nirvanic level. The human beings become, in some future world, divine incarnations.

3. Enter into the so-called spiritual phase, and forget everything that concerns the Earth.

4. Become a very efficient and invisible collaborator of humanity.

5. Become a member of the occult Hierarchy

that governs and protects the world in which they reach perfection.

6. Become part of the chain of future worlds, to help build their forms.

7. Enter the angelic evolution of the devas.[23]

8. Consecrate oneself to the immediate service of the Logos, in some part of the Solar System, to be used by It as Minister and Messenger.

9. The spiritual evolution of the internal and immortal man constitutes the fundamental doctrine of the occult sciences. And to understand all of this, the student must believe in the One Universal Life, independent of matter, and in the individual Intelligences that animate the different manifestations of this principle."

---

23 Beings with an evolutionary line parallel to that of humanity. They do not have dense physical bodies. See ESOTERIC LEXICON.

"Universal fraternity has as its base the common soul. It is because there is a common soul for all of humanity that fraternity, or even a common understanding, is possible. If we make humans base themselves upon this foundation they will be saved. There is a divine power in each human being, which rules its life and which nobody can influence towards evil—not even the greatest magician. Let human beings place their lives under this guidance and they will not have anything to fear from any human being or from the devil."

H.P. Blavatsky
(excerpt from a talk)

Bibliographical References

- AGNI YOGA. New York: Agni Yoga Society, 1954.

- H. P. Blavatsky. THE SECRET DOCTRINE—The Synthesis of Science, Religion and Philosophy, Volume I. Theosophical Publishing House, Wheaton, IL 1993.

- H. P. Blavatsky. THE SECRET DOCTRINE—The Synthesis of Science, Religion and Philosophy, Volume II, Theosophical Publishing House, Wheaton, IL 1993.

- H. P. Blavatsky. THE SECRET DOCTRINE—The Synthesis of Science, Religion and Philosophy, Volume III. Theosophical Publishing House, Wheaton, IL 1993.

- H. P. Blavatsky. THE VOICE OF THE SILENCE. Theosophical Publishing House, Wheaton, IL 1982.

- H. P. Blavatsky. THE THEOSOPHICAL GLOSSARY. Theosophical Publishing House, Wheaton, IL.

- J. Trigueirinho Netto. ERKS (THE INNER WORLD). Sao Paulo, Brazil: Editora Pensamento.

- J. Trigueirinho Netto. ESOTERIC GLOSSARY. Sao Paulo, Brazil: Editora Pensamento.

- J. Trigueirinho Netto. MIZ TLI TLAN – A WORLD THAT AWAKENS. Sao Paulo, Brazil: Editora Pensamento.

- S. Cranston. H.P.B.: The Extraordinary Life and Influence of Helena Blavatsky. Founder of the Modern Theosophical Movement. Tarcher, New York 1993.

About Trigueirinho and His Work

Jose Trigueirinho Netto (1931-2018) was born in Sao Paulo, Brazil. He lived in Europe for a number of years, where he maintained contact with individuals who were advanced on the spiritual path, including Paul Brunton.

In his own life he was an example of the teachings that he transmitted through his books and talks about the transcendence and elevation of the human being, the contact with the soul and with even more profound nuclei of the being, impersonal service, and the link with the Spiritual Hierarchies.

One of the fundamental elements of his work is to stimulate the expansion of human consciousness and to liberate it from the bonds that keep it imprisoned to material aspects of existence, both external and internal.

He was the Founder of the Community of Light Figueira (http://www.comunidadefigueira.org.br) and a Founder and member of the Board of Directors of the Fraternity International Humanitarian Federation (www.fraterinternacional) as well as a Co-Founder of the Grace Mercy Order, an ecumenical Christian monastic order. He also was an active collaborator, instructor and spiritual protector of three other communities located in Uruguay, Argentina and Portugal.

In his last 30 years he lived in the Community of Light Figueira, in the interior of Minas Gerais, Brazil, a community that at present has approximately 300 residents and which is visited annually by thousands of collaborators who are members of a larger network of humanitarian services and of spiritual studies that was always guided and followed closely by Trigueirinho.

Thanks to his inestimable instruction and his love for the Kingdoms of Nature and as a result of the exemplary work that he himself implanted in the Figueira community, the Animal, Vegetable and Mineral Kingdoms are the recipients of loving treatment there.

Trigueirinho wrote over 80 books, published originally in Portuguese, with many of them translated into Spanish, English, French and German. He gave more than 3,000 talks that were recorded live and which are available in CD, with some available in DVD and pen drive.

The primary focus of the first phase of Trigueirinho's work was concerned with self-knowledge, prayer, instruction and spiritual transformation. Following this, he began to transmit information with respect to Universal Life and about the assistance that humanity has from its beginnings received by means of the Intra-terrestrial White Brotherhood which inhabits the Retreats and the Planetary Centers as well as through the Cosmic Brotherhood of the Universe. He provides information about the presence of the Spiritual Hierarchy on the planet and the advent of the new humanity.

His work also includes themes relating to: the need for humanity to balance the negative karmas that it has created in relation to the Kingdoms of Nature; the negative karmic burden that we carry from the history of slavery and the genocide of indigenous peoples; and the nature of spiritual work in groups. He also addresses issues of healing, a larger vision of astrology, the esoteric nature of symbols, sound and colors, and the divine feminine.

In his last eight years he analyzed with clarity and with the wisdom that always characterized him, the messages that the Divinity has been giving to the planet as a warning to humanity (available from www.mensajerosdivinos.org/en).

His work reveals a real comprehension of the significance of all the Kingdoms of Nature on our planet, the true spiritual task of the human being, its place in the universe and also its responsibility before Creation.

Finally, he clarifies the reasons for the crisis that today is devastating humanity, teaching how to avoid reacting negatively to an immanent natural catastrophe by contacting more subtle levels of consciousness, and opening perspectives for the beginning of a more luminous cycle for our race.

Books by Trigueirinho

(Books available in English have English title first)

Published by Editora Pensamento
Sao Paulo, Brazil

1987

NOSSA VIDA NOS SONHOS
OUR LIFE IN DREAMS

A ENERGIA DOS RAIOS EM NOSSA VIDA
THE ENERGY OF THE RAYS IN OUR LIVES

1988

DO IRREAL AO REAL
FROM THE UNREAL TO THE REAL

HORA DE CRESCER INTERIORMENTE
O Mito de Hércules Hoje
TIME FOR INNER GROWTH – *The Myth of Hercules Today*

A MORTE SEM MEDO E SEM CULPA
DEATH WITHOUT FEAR AND WITHOUT GUILT

CAMINHOS PARA A CURA INTERIOR
PATHS TO INNER HEALING

1989

ERKS – *Mundo Interno*
ERKS – *The Inner World*

Miz Tli Tlan – *Um Mundo que Desperta*
MIZ TLI TLAN – *A World that Awakens*

Aurora – Essência Cósmica Curadora
AURORA – *Cosmic Essence of Healing*

Signs of Contact
SINAIS DE CONTATO

O Novo Começo do Mundo
THE NEW BEGINNING OF THE WORLD

A Quinta Raça
THE FIFTH RACE

Padrões de conduta para a nova Humanidade
PATTERNS OF CONDUCT FOR THE NEW HUMANITY

Novos Sinais de Contato
NEW SIGNS OF CONTACT

Os Jardineiros do Espaço
THE SPACE GARDENERS

1990

A Busca da Síntese
THE SEARCH FOR SYNTHESIS

Noah's Vessel
A NAVE DE NOÉ

Tempo de Retiro e Tempo de Vigília
A TIME OF RETREAT AND A TIME OF VIGIL

1991

Portas do Cosmos
GATEWAYS OF THE COSMOS

Encontro Interno – *A Consciência-Nave*
INNER ENCOUNTER – *The Consciousness Space Vessel*

A Hora do Resgate
THE TIME OF RESCUE

O Livro Dos Sinais
THE BOOK OF SIGNS

Mirna Jad – *Santuário Interior*
MIRNA JAD – *Inner Sanctuary*

As Chaves de Ouro
THE GOLDEN KEYS

1992

Das Lutas à Paz
FROM STRUGGLE TO PEACE

A Morada Dos Elisíos
THE ELYSIAN DWELLING PLACE

Hora de Curar – *A Existência Oculta*
TIME FOR HEALING – *The Occult Existence*

O Ressurgimento de Fátima Lis
THE RESURGENCE OF FATIMA LIS

HISTÓRIA ESCRITA NOS ESPELHOS
Princípios de Comunicação Cósmic
HISTORY WRITTEN IN THE MIRRORS -
Principles of Cosmic Communication

PASSOS ATUAIS
STEPS FOR NOW

VIAGEM POR MUNDOS SUTIS
TRAVEL THROUGH SUBTLE WORLDS

SEGREDOS DESVELADOS – *Iberah e Anu Tea*
UNVEILED SECRETS – *Iberah and Anu Tea*

A CRIAÇÃO – *Nos Caminhos da Energia*
CREATION – *On the Paths of Energy*

THE MYSTERY OF THE CROSS IN THE PRESENT PLANETARY TRANSITION
O MISTÉRIO DA CRUZ NA ATUAL TRANSIÇÃO PLANETÁRIA

O NASCIMENTO DA HUMANIDADE FUTURA
THE BIRTH OF THE FUTURE HUMANITY

1993

AOS QUE DESPERTAM
TO THOSE WHO AWAKEN

PAZ INTERNA EM TEMPOS CRÍTICOS
INNER PEACE IN CRITICAL TIMES

A FORMAÇÃO DE CURADORES
THE FORMATION OF HEALERS

Profecias aos Que Não Temem Dizer Sim
PROPHECIES FOR THOSE WHO ARE NOT AFRAID TO SAY YES

The Voice of Amhaj
A VOZ DE AMHAJ

O Visitante – O Caminho Para Anu Tea
THE VISITOR —*The Way to Anu Tea*

A Cura da Humanidade
THE HEALING OF HUMANITY

Os Números e a Vidas – *Uma Nova Compreensão da Simbologia Oculta nos Números*
NUMBERS AND LIFE – *A New Understanding of Occult Symbolism in Numbers*

Niskalkat – *Uma Mensagem para os Tempos de Emergência*
NISKALKAT – *A Message for Times of Emergency*

Encontros Com a Paz
ENCOUNTERS WITH PEACE

Novos Oráculos
NEW ORACLES

Um Novo Impulso Astrológico
A NEW ASTROLOGICAL IMPULSE

1994

Bases do Mundo Ardente – *Indicações para Contato com os Mundos suprafíscicos*

BASES OF THE FIERY WORLD – *Indications for Contacts with Suprapyhsical Worlds*

CONTATOS COM UM MONASTÉRIO INTERATERRENO
CONTACTS WITH AN INTRATERRESTRIAL MONASTERY

OS OCEANOS TÊM OUVIDOS
OCEANS HAVE EARS

A TRAJETÓRIA DO FOGO
THE PATH OF FIRE

GLOSSÁRIO ESOTÉRICO
ESOTERIC LEXICON

1995

THE LIGHT WITHIN YOU
A LUZ DENTRO DE TI

1996

DOORWAY TO A KINGDOM
PORTAL PARA UM REINO

BEYOND KARMA
ALÉM DO CARMA

1997

WE ARE NOT ALONE
NÃO ESTAMOS SÓS

WINDS OF THE SPIRIT
VENTOS DO ESPÍRITO

Finding the Temple
O ENCONTRO DO TEMPLO

There is Peace
A PAZ EXISTE

1998

Path Without Shadows
CAMINHO SEM SOMBRAS

Mensagens para Uma Vida de Harmonia
MESSAGES FOR A LIFE OF HARMONY

1999

Toque Divino
THE DIVINE TOUCH

Coleçào Pedaços de Céu
BITS FROM HEAVEN COLLECTION
- **Aromas do Espaço**
  AROMAS FROM SPACE
- **Nova Vida Bate à Porta**
  A NEW LIFE AWAITS YOU
- **Mais Luz No Horizonte**
  MORE LIGHT ON THE HORIZON
- **O Campanário Cósmico**
  THE COSMIC CAMPANILE
- **Nada Nos Falta**
  WE LACK NOTHING
- **Sagrados Mistérios**
  SACRED MYSTERIES

- **ILHAS DE SALVAÇÃO**
  ISLANDS OF SALVATION

2002

CALLING HUMANITY
UM CHAMADO ESPECIAL

2004

ÉS VIAJANTE CÓSMICO
YOU ARE A COSMIC WAYFARER

IMPULSOS
IMPULSES

2005

PENSAMENTOS PARA TODO O ANO
THOUGHTS FOR THE WHOLE YEAR

2006

TRABALHO ESPIRITUAL COM A MENTE
SPIRITUAL WORK WITH THE MIND

Published by Editora Irdin
Carmo da Cachoeira, Minas Gerais, Brazil

2009

SIGNS OF BLAVATSKY – *An Unusual Encounter for the Present Time*

SINAIS DE BLAVATSKY – *Um Inusitado Encontro nos Dias de Hoje*

2012

Consciências e Hierarquias
CONSCIOUSNESSES AND HIERARCHIES

2015

Mensagens Reunidas
COLLECTED MESSAGES

Mensagens para Sua Tranformaçã
MESSAGES FOR YOUR TRANSFORMATION

2017

Páginas de Amor e Compreensão
PAGES OF LOVE AND COMPREHENSION

2018

Novos Tempos: Nova Postura
NEW TIMES: NEW ATTITUDE

2020

Versos Livres
OBRA PÓSTUMA

Trigueirinho's works are published by:

Associação Irdin Editora – www.irdin.org.br (selected titles of books in English, Spanish and Portuguese and CDs in several languages), Carmo da Cachoeira, MG, Brazil.

Editora Pensamento – www.pensamento-cultrix.com.br (titles in Portuguese), São Paulo, SP, Brazil

Editorial Kier – www.kier.com.ar (selected titles in Spanish), Buenos Aires, Argentina.

Lichtwelle-Verlag – www.lichtwelle-verlag.ch (selected titles in Spanish and German), Zurich, Switzerland.

Shasti Association – www.shasti.org (selected titles in English), Mount Shasta, CA, USA